Escaping from the Evil

Escaping from the Evil

Caption: **Annie T Djoum 6 years after her escape from the evil.**

Annie T. Djoum

Library of Congress Control Number:		2011901843
ISBN:	Hardcover	978-1-4568-6489-7
	Softcover	978-1-4568-6488-0
	Ebook	978-1-4568-6490-3

This book was printed in the United States of America.

To order additional copies of this book, contact:
Xlibris Corporation
1-888-795-4274
www.Xlibris.com
Orders@Xlibris.com
91213

Contents

This Book is dedicated

to my children Ange and Ryan who were there to give me the strength to continue to live during my struggle with the evil and my battle to escape from the evil

to my mother Jeannette Kossi and my father Joseph Tcheute who believed in me, for the affection and attention and also for their support to my education and help they brought me to set up a plan to escape the evil.

to my grandmother Margueritte Simo who came to the US in Emergency to help me during my divorce and custody battle with the evil. Thank to my grandmother who helped me to raise my children and to finish with my studies.

I will also like to thank my sister Liliane Kom and her partner Calvin Njampou for their love and their help.

I will like to thank my Friend Dr. Anne Marie Moukala Cadet for her sincere attention, advice and friendship.

I am finally dedicated this book to women over the world who leave in abusive relationship especially African women to be able to take action and step out of from the misery to save their life.

Preface

I start to write this book in 2004 when I was taking a speech class. I wrote this book because I was in a very abusive relationship and this was my way to express what I was living and feeling while working an escape plan with my children. The trouble that I encountered in writing this book was that as a new immigrant of the U.S.A, I was in a new country that I like without family member or strong support group. One of my concern was also to escape with my children without fighting with their father.

I am also writing this book to women who are victim of domestique violence and abuse by their partner to be able to escape instead of losing their life or their dignity.

Statistics have also shown that Domestic Violence is the leading cause of injury to women between the ages of 15 and 44 in the United States, more than car accidents, muggings and rapes combined. (Violence against women, a majority staff report, "Committee on the judiciary, United States Senate, 102 nd Congress, October 1992, P.3)

By researching on this topic, I have also found that an estimated 1.3 million women are victims of physical assault by an intimate partner each year. (Costs of Intimate partner Violence Against Women in the United States 2003. Center for Disease Control and Prevention, National Center for Injury Prevention and Control, Atlanta, GA.

The average prison sentence of men who kill their women partners is 2 to 6 years. Women who kill their partner are, on average sentenced to 15 years (National Coalition Against Domestic Violence, 1989)

Boys who witness domestic violence are twice as likely to abuse their own partners and children when they become adults. (Strauss, Gelles and Smith, " Physical Violence in America families. Transaction Publishers 1990)

Acknowledgment

I would like to sincerely acknowledge the contribution of my daughter Ange Guianin and my cousin Christelle Yombah who prodived me with valuable assistance in prepararing this book. I will also like to thank my friend Dr. Anne—Marie Moukala Cadet for her advises and support during my preparation of this book.

Introduction

I believed—and I still believe—that marriage or having a partner is a strong foundation for life and society. When I went to study medicine in Belgium, I experienced loneliness. Even if I was 60 percent sure that my marriage with the parent of my children will not work, I decided to bring him to the USA, the country of my dreams, against my parents' will. I put the interest of the children and my happiness first.

I knew that the sky is the limit for people who have big dreams and who are willing to work hard to achieve their dream in the USA.

I also believed that people who are educated are open-minded and tolerant to diversity and different cultures. I brought the father of my children because I needed a trustable and believable friend and partner in this country, where people like their comfort zone and where the culture is different from the one in my native country. In my country, someone can visit friends and family members without appointment. I never lived for a long time with the evil in Cameroon; I knew him well in the USA when I lived with him in the same house. Without my family's help (mother, father, grandmother, sister, and children), I would not have been alive today.

This relationship was deteriorating because of many factors, like educational difference, the incompatibility in the vision of acceptable social values and norms, his lack of respect to me and my parents, his dishonest and very controlling behavior.

In the next line, I would describe my life with the evil and how I escaped from him.

Chapter 1:
Where I Met the Evil

In Cameroon, my native country, I used to go visit my cousin in the city of Douala. During one of those visits, my cousin Mimi, along with some of her friends, invited me to a nightclub. I went to the nightclub and met the evil. He invited me the first time to dance with him. I refused. After the second attempt, we exchanged our contact information, which were our cell phone numbers. He told me that he lived in the city of Bafoussam. My mother and my father lived in the same city. At that time, I used to visit my parents two weekends a month because I was student at the University of Dschang-Cameroon.

**Annie T Djoum working on her master thesis at the
Univesity of Dschang in Cameroon**

Chapter 2:
Living with the Evil in Cameroon

After many dates with the evil, he used to visit me some weekends at the university, where I lived on the campus.

There are many theories that explain the root of the relationship between people. One of these theories are the interpersonal needs theory, William Shutz, explaining this theory, says that relationships are started, built, and maintained on the basis of how well each person meets the interpersonal needs of the other: affection need (a desire to express and receive love), inclusion need (a share to be in the company of other people), and control need (a desire to influence the events and people around us). Another theory is the exchange theory introduced by J. W. Thibaut and H. H. Kelly, which proposes that relationships can be understood in terms of the exchange of rewards and costs that take place during individual's interactions. Rewards are outcomes that are valued by a person, and costs are outcomes that a person does not wish to incur.

Because I am someone very patient, who believes that people can know each other better with time and can therefore try to meet their partner's interpersonal needs when they know each other better, I am always not too much expectant at the beginning of a relationship. In my case, with X, when I met him, I told him that I was a student at the University of Dschang (Cameroon) and that I was working on my master's thesis; I also told him that I went to study medicine in Belgium and that I came back to Cameroon because I was sick.

During the first year of our relationship, I lived at the university's campus, and he came to visit me one weekend per month. At that time, I did not need him to be around me too much because I was working on my master's thesis. What made me mad was that when he came to visit me, he did not even bring me a present.

In 2002, I won the Green Card Lottery to immigrate in the USA, my dream's country. The evil and I got our daughter, Ange. A few months after my daughter and I got the visa to immigrate in the USA, the evil came to see my parents to talk about marriage. Because of my daughter and because of my second pregnancy, I did not say no to the union, even though I knew that he was not a good person. I did say yes to the marriage because I needed a friend and partner in this country far away from my family (USA); and also, based on my religious believes, I did not want to abort.

After my nonsense marriage to the evil, the marriage reception was at my parents' house. The evil did not even plan anything for the marriage. He went in hiding in the townhouse to do the publication of benches, because he knew that he was a bad person and that people who knew him will tell me or my parents to stop the marriage. I also remembered that the evil usually visited me at night, and he did not want to visit me during daytime, because he did not want people who knew him well to tell my family who he was. I also remembered that during my graduation ceremony from the university, the evil was not supportive of my studies. He came to the graduation ceremony the night before my graduation; and he did not even sleep at Dschang, the university's city and where the graduation was taking place, to help me to set up and organize my graduation ceremony. My sister Liliane was the one who helped me with everything. He came to the graduation after everything was over at the school. He showed up only for the party section of the graduation. When I was complaining, he did not even want to listen. I also remembered my grandmother asking me why my partner was not there. One of my teachers whom I worked on my master's thesis with also asked me, "Where is your fiancé?" My lack of experience and maturity did not make me see that I was dealing with the evil.

Chapter 3:
The Airport Scenes

I will talk about this point so that many things that I will talk about in the next lines can be clarified and easy to understand. One year after I met the evil, I became pregnant with my daughter, Ange. He came to present himself to my parents when I was five months pregnant. Since that time, he never talked about engagement or marriage to me or my parents. I was still at the university. Clara, a student at the same university with me, was introduced to me by my sister Liliane and was one of Liliane's friends. Clara came from the University of Buea in Cameroon, where English is the main language of study. In fact, my native country, Cameroon, is a bilingual country. I was living with Clara on the campus, and I was sharing my bed with her. I was also helping Clara with the class material that was in French by translating it to English for her. After a while, I talked to Clara that I was looking for a scholarship because I wanted to go to a country with better opportunities after my master's thesis to do MD and PhD studies. Clara, one day, brought the green card material to me; I played and won.

After I won the Green Card Lottery, the evil came frequently to see my parents and talked about marriage. In April 2002, my daughter Ange and I got the immigrant visa. The evil and I got married in July 2002. The evil did not have the visa because we were not married by the time I went to my interview at the embassy. Because we were married, the evil told to my parents that he would pay for my travel ticket to come to the USA and that they don't have to worry about nothing. I called some of my friends and family members, my sister's friends and family members, and my aunt's friends and family members to tell them the date that I would travel. The evil told my family that we have to go to the city of Douala, where I was supposed to take the airplane on Friday, July 19, 2002. Before that day, the evil and I had had contact on the phone, and he reassured me that everything about the trip was good. I arrived in the city of Douala on Thursday with my sisters. My mother and father and my grandmother arrived on Friday. I called the evil on Thursday because I needed the money to buy the travel bag. He sent me to see a friend where I would have the money. He reassured me that he bought my airport ticket. He was the only one who knew that I was pregnant with my son. On Friday, family members and parents and friends came to the airport because I was traveling.

I did not go to the airport because I suspected that he would not show up. In fact, I had been calling him during the day, and he did not pick up the phone. People that went to the airport waited for him there until 11:00 p.m. to come with the travel ticket, the time that the airplane was supposed to fly. This event was a shame to me and my parents, friends, sisters, and family members. I was so ashamed and morally down that I did not show up at the airport. The evil knew that I was four months pregnant, and by acting like that, the evil wanted to kill me. Parents and friends and family members came to support me after the airport incident. My uncle and family members told me to call the embassy and asked them not to give him the visa to come to the USA. Unfortunately, it was already too late for me because I have already been trapped by signing the marriage certificate. Another element was that he was the only one who knew that I was four months pregnant.

On Sunday, July 21, 2002, my sister bought my ticket; and I travelled to the country of my dream with a lower spirit and state of mind. My family decided before I travelled that I would not let the evil come to the USA and I would never call the evil, but I called him two weeks after I arrived in the USA. I called him because he was the father of my daughter, and I was pregnant with my second son with him. Only he and I knew that I was pregnant when I left Cameroon. Even my mother and father did not know. Because my dream was to have children who would be raised by their mother and father so that they could have all the attention and affection they needed to grow up, I decided that I would forgive him for that. I sent an invitation letter to the evil so that he could come in the USA as a visitor. The other reason that made me let him come here was that my daughter was still at home, and at that time, her visa was about to expire. My family was upset about my decision, but I wanted to be here with my daughter, and I was already trapped by the marriage certificate that I had signed.

Another point was that it was an important life decision, because in order for me to completely end my relationship with the father of my children, I had to think maturely. I was also dreaming of a family's life and to have children that will be raised by their two parents. By bringing him to the USA, I was trying to have a partner, and it was scary for me to be alone in a new country without family members. It was also an occasion for me to know him better because it was the first time that we lived together in the same house. I remembered one of my mother's uncles whom I presented the evil to in Cameroon told me three times, "I hope that after working hard all those years to get your opportunity, the evil will not kill you to steal your hard work." I have also learned later that the evil told his friends that he has trapped me with the marriage certificate and the second pregnancy and that he wanted only to use me and mess up my life with the children. He said to people that he wanted only the green card, that he did not love me.

Chapter 4:
The Lies of the Evil

When I met the evil in 2001, he told me that he had a PhD in architecture and that he went to school to Canada. What really attracted me to become his girlfriend was that he was a doctor in architecture, because I like to have close relationships with people who are educated. My reason for this choice is that my life's experience showed me that educated people are open-minded, very understanding, and they are very tolerant and sociable because of their background and cultural diversity. Later on, friends told me that he was not an architect and that he has been suspended in the architect registry in Cameroon because he had lied about his credentials. Moreover, most of the construction works that he had done in Cameroon were poorly done.

Another lie of the evil is when I called him the day before I traveled to the airport and he reassured me that he was in the town of Douala. Later on, he told my parents that he was in a town named Eseka with one of his best friends and was stuck in traffic because a tree was felled on his way. Some days later, my uncles told me that the night of the day that I was travelling, he was in a nightclub in the city of Bafoussam in Cameroon. The third lie of the evil was during the custody battle at the courthouse in the USA, where he lied to the judge at the beginning of the hearing that he was not working because he was undocumented. Later on, at the end of the hearing, he told to the judge that he was not going to CASA of Maryland anymore because he was getting contractor work and was hiring people to work for him. He told all those lies because he did not want to pay the child support money for the children. The fourth lie of the evil was about him telling people that he was the one who played my lottery. My question is, why did he not play on his own? The fifth lie of the evil was during the

child-support hearing, when he told to the judge that he had no home and that he was sleeping on a chair that he was renting in an apartment. In fact, three weeks after I escaped from the evil, his girlfriend that he was hanging out with moved in the apartment that I rented when I came to the USA. The last lie of the evil was in court, when he told to his lawyer that I had cut my son's feet. The truth is that because he knew that I have escaped with the children, he was so frustrated because he knew that I will not give him the green card. He had plotted with my children's pediatrician and the first lawyer that I have hired for the divorce for them to find a way to put me in jail.

Chapter 5:
My Arrival in the USA.

After the evil did not show up at the Airport in Douala, Cameroon, my sister Liliane borrowed some money and paid for my travel ticket for me to go to Paris where my aunt lives. My aunt Henriette and Clara were there waiting for me to spend some time with them before I travelled to the country of my dreams. I called my cousin Caroline because I needed a place to live for some time. I arrived in Paris and spent three weeks with my aunts Henriette and Clara. They paid for my travel ticket for me to come to the USA.

I arrived here on August 8, 2002. I have been living with my cousin Caroline for two months; before the father of my children came with my daughter, I had been looking for an apartment and for a job. I was able to get a cleaning job at CASA of Maryland. Moreover, I was also able to gather some information and resources for the evil, the children, and me. Later on, I went to the social service to apply for the TCA and food stamps and to get resources for a job. I was able to get addresses and applications for apartment buildings.

For the process of my integration in the USA, I started to take some English classes in Montgomery County in Maryland because my first language is French. I was also able to take the nursing assistant test. Later on, I took the test for me to be able to work at Red Lobster Restaurant. After some weeks with the ESOL classes with the county, I found out that I was at the wrong place and that my level was higher than where I was. I decided to go to Montgomery College to take the LOEP exam (English placement exam). I took the LOEP exam and was placed in EL 102 and RD 101.

Chapter 6:
Living with the Evil in the USA

The father of my children came to the USA in October of 2002 with my daughter, Ange. We lived at my cousin's house for three weeks. After those three weeks, we were able to get a bedroom as roommates. I went with the evil at a day labor working center in Silver Spring, Maryland. He was able to get daily job and started to have some income. We stayed as roommates for two months. After those two months, I was able to get a one-bedroom apartment where I lived with the evil and my daughter. In December of 2002, my son came to the world in a hospital in Maryland.

I used to pay half of the rent because I was working as a *bosser* in a Restaurant in Silver Spring, Maryland. The evil took the Comcast Cable in my name, and I was responsible to pay the bill; I was also responsible of the food.

I went to Montgomery College in January of 2003, one month after the birth of my son. I was the one who was dropping the children at the day care.

When it comes to the inclusion needs, which is the desire to be in the company of other people, the evil does not have close friends at all: he has only occasional friends. During my relationship with him, at that time until now, I was never presented to his family. We visited one of his friends when he came to the USA, and that relationship today is over because he always likes to use people. To be specific, when he is friends with someone, he tries to gain something from him. When that person notices what type of person he is, he would stop the relationship by divulging bad thoughts about that person to people who know him. In my case, I really like to invite friends and cook for them on special occasions like birthdays, Christmas, and Thanksgiving. During Thanksgiving of 2005, I invited my cousin—the one who gave me a place to sleep when I came to the USA—with some of her friends to my apartment. In fact, my cousin also supported the evil when he came to the USA. To be specific, when he came to the USA, he lived at my cousin's house for two weeks before we moved. After the ceremony, I told him that I had spent a hundred dollars for the festivity. He was upset, asking me how I could spend so much money for my cousin. I was shocked about his behavior because when I came here, I lived with my cousin for two months, not paying for rent or food. She helped him the same way that she helped me when he came to this country. By inviting my cousin, I wanted to thank her for all things she had done for me.

Talking about the cost of investment of time and money, I never had any of those since I had been with the evil; he went to the movie with me only one time in Cameroon, and at that time, he had a free ticket. He did not even remember to wish me happy birthday. Even to go to the mall with me, he always avoided to go shopping with me because he was afraid that he will spend some money. One year ago, I bought him a present for his birthday, but I never received one from him. I sometimes invited him to the restaurant to show him what it means to have good manners, but he would never do the same thing.

At the beginning of my relationship with the evil, I was thinking that my affection need, which is the desire to express and receive love, was satisfied; but this was just an illusion. Because I always express my affection and my attachment to people, I notice that I face the problem of abuse by those people that I love too much, especially friends and men with whom I have sexual relationships with. The point is that I notice that in this world, there are too few people who know to appreciate attention and affection that someone brings to them. Most of the people think that when you are kind to them, it is because they are more important than you and you are just being forced to be their friend. I think that this was and this is still what the evil thought. He also thought that I cannot live without him. For the verbal affection, I will definitively say that I never really received a sincere one. When it comes to the nonverbal affection, I have been abused physically by the evil.

Talking about the control needs, at that time, he showed me a behavior that demonstrated he was a person who needed to lead at certain times but contented to follow the lead of others at other times. But sometimes, I was frustrated by his dictatorial and nonlistening behavior. For example, one day, we were watching the television with some of his friends And one French rock singer named Johnny Hallyday were presented. The evil said that he was seventy years old, and I told him that he was sixty-one. I explained to him that I could not forget Johnny's age, because he was born the same year as my father. He was upset because I gave something different from what he said and started telling me that I know nothing and that he knew better than me about Johnny. He did all this in the presence of his friends. I was very upset, and I told him that I would bring a magazine the next day, which showed Johnny's age. Another remark is that when you try to give him some advice; he will reject your offer by telling you that he does not need advice from anyone.

Also, because I wanted to improve my life and to succeed in this country, when I got my son, I begged my mother to come and help us. She agreed to come to the USA to help us. My mother came to the USA, and I was able to work without any concern that I had to drop or pick up the children to the day care center. He was, therefore, able to buy his first car. Moreover, when my father came to the USA, he bought his second car. I am the one who brought groceries to the house by bus. When I bought my car, he was jealous and asked his mechanic not to fix my car for the inspection. He also called the towing company to tow my car, which was parked in the complex where we used to live together.

I filed for the evil to have his green card in 2003. The evil is very irresponsible that he does not want to have a cell phone because he knows that I can call him if the children are sick or if I need help. During the day, I am not in communication with him because I do not know how to reach him. He rarely calls me on my cell phone during the day to know if I need something.

In this relationship, my reward is the humiliation that I receive from the evil. I am very ashamed of this relationship because of the environment that I was raised in and the type of education that I received from my parents; this is a big failure for me because when my mother was here, she always asked me, "Where did you meet this type of person?" My father asked me the same question. During my mother's stay with us, he lacked respect for her and sometimes even insulted her. He did the same thing to my father. I was also beaten many times by the evil during our marriage. One time was when I told him that once he got his green card, we would divorce; the other time was when I refused to have sex with him because I felt like he was just using me. In this relationship, I think that I have no rewards at all and that I made the biggest mistake of my life to be with the evil.

I always dream to live peacefully with someone, where we will listen to each other, but that is not the case in this relationship. The evil is someone who does not like criticism or dialogue. He wants people to listen to him because he pretends that he knows everything better than others. Even in a conversation, he just wants to talk alone and does not give others the chance to talk. Also, he lies too much, like he lied to me that he was a doctor. In fact, I have never seen any of his degrees or credentials. I have also noticed that by observing the evil closely, I see that he does not even have a high school diploma. Also, he is very messy: my bedroom was always messy, and he was using the entire closet as if I had no right to have my own space. When I was not at home, he will pry into my things to know everything that I am doing. In this relationship, the conflict happens at least on time every month. If It happens that we are calm at home, he tries to attack my father and me; I think there is nothing I can do to save this relationship because it is affecting me morally, psychologically, and even physically in a negative way.

Chapter 7:
My Mother's Visit to the USA.

My son Ryan was born in 2002. Because as a new immigrant of the USA, a country that I felt in love with, because of all the opportunities that were available to people who were willing to work hard, I decided that I would live here with my children. I sent an invitation letter to my mother for her to come to the USA. My mother came in 2003; at that time, I was going to school full time and was also braiding hair in a salon. My mother helped the evil and me to take care of our children.

During my mother's stay, the relationship between the evil and I was full of conflicts and tension because we did not understand each other and he was very controlling, financially. He had no respect or appreciation for the help that my mother was giving us to raise our children. I was working very hard to support the family because he was undocumented. My mother was cooking for us. She was also taking care of the children and the laundry. I also remember that the evil bought a tape recorder that he was hiding in the living room for him to be able to record all the conversations that my mother and I would have.

The question and the concern that I am asking myself is that why he was afraid of my mother and me if he did not have evil plans about me. I thought that marriage should be a relationship of love, happiness, and trust between two people. I think that his plan to kill and hurt me was in effect for a long time.

My mother stayed with us for five months. When my mother went back to Cameroon, I was the one who paid for her travel ticket. The evil did not even buy her a present to thank her for all her free hard work that she had done during her stay in the USA. I also remember that when my mother was going back to Cameroon, he did not even go to the airport to tell her good-bye.

29

My mother's visit to the U.S.A

Chapter 8:
My Mother Went Back to Cameroon

After my mother return to Cameroon, she talked to my father about the misery that I was living in with the evil. I also used to call them to tell them that I was very unhappy in my marriage with the evil. My mother, father, and I started to plan what we could do. I was very sick in my body because I was working, going to school, and raising the children. In 2004, I called my mother because I needed extra help. I wanted her to come to the USA again.

**Annie T Djoum with aunt Henriette Makambeu during
my aunt visit to the U.S.A.**

Chapter 9:
My Aunt's Visit to the USA

My aunt Henriette came to visit me in 2003 in the USA. After her stay with me for a while, she used her experience as an adult to notice that I was in a very destructive marriage and that I was already trapped by the evil. She stayed with us for one month. Before she left the USA, she recommended me to one of her friends named Roger to help me in case I need help and to be with me to listen to my concerns. Roger was very helpful because he used to visit us and see how I was living. Roger was also very helpful during my custody battle with the evil because he was the only trustable friend that I had at that time. Most of my friends were gone, because as a divorced single mother, they thought that I could be in financial hardship and would ask them for some help. All of them were gone. Roger was also the one who helped me when my car was broken to pick up the children from the day care center.

Annie T Djoum's father, Joseph Tcheute during his visit in the U.S.A before my escape from the evil.

Annie's father Joseph Tcheute with children Ange and Ryan after the children been picked up from the baby sitter by my father during my stay with the evil.

Chapter 10:
My Father's Visit to the USA

After many talks with my mother, we came to the conclusion that my mother should come. I called my father and talked about that with him. He accepted and said that he would come. I sent an invitation letter to my father to come to the USA. He went to the embassy of the USA in Cameroon and got a visa. I bought my father a travel ticket for him to come to the USA. My father came to the USA. The day that my father came, the evil did not even go to the airport to welcome my father. I went to the airport by myself and brought my father home.

After my father's arrival in the USA, my father helped me with the children by dropping them and picking them up at the babysitter's. I remember that the evil was making fun of my work and my studies by telling to my father that her daughter was working as a bosser in a restaurant. He was also making fun of my studies at Montgomery College by telling my father and friends that I study English at Montgomery College and that it will bring me nowhere. During my father's stay, the evil was making fun of my father by telling him that he knows that he came to the USA for a mission. My father, who had high blood pressure, used to suffer a lot during his stay with us because the evil will create conflict—and my father blood pressure will go up.

My father came to the USA. I was able to finish my driving class that I started when my mother was in the USA. While going to Montgomery College, I was also able to take some nursing assistant classes that I paid for with the money that I got at my restaurant job. I got my license as a certified nursing assistant (CNA). I took the board exam and got my GNA license. During my father's stay with us, I was able to get a nursing assistant job and also able to buy my first car.

My father approved my decision that I had to go. The evil was very afraid when my father came to the USA because he knew that my father will help me make a decision. I also remember that the evil went to my children's babysitter and told her that she didn't have to take care of the children anymore. The children, at that time, stayed at home. The TV that I bought, the evil sold it, and we were at home without a TV. My father was at home for two months with the children, who used to go to the babysitter.

I also remembered that all the items in the house—and I was the one who bought them—were thrown away by the evil.

During all the tension, I started to look at affordable apartments in Montgomery County; after six months of intensive search, I was able to find an apartment. The evil did not know nothing about it. I also remember that during all those six months, all my clothes and items were taken out of the closet and put on the floor in the room. The evil, by that act, wanted to tell me that I have to go.

I also remember that the evil, one day, poured my father food on the floor and told us that this was just a warning. I also remember that that day, I called the police.

My daughter Ange with son Ryan at Ryan birthday party 2 years after my escape from the evil.

**My son Ryan birthday with daughter
Ange after my escape from the evil.**

Chapter 11:
My Escape from the Evil

In 2003, my father and I started to plan how to escape with the children. I talked to a friend about the abusive situation and the misery that my father and I were living with. She advised me to get a lawyer. She gave me her lawyer's phone number. I called him and made an appointment. I saw the lawyer and talked to him about the verbal and physical abuse that my father and I were going through. He told me that I have to pay one thousand dollars for the divorce process. He asked me to give him three hundred dollars as first payment. I gave him eight hundred dollars total and requested the receipt that I did not get. He wanted the money in cash. The lawyer took my money and did not file for my case.

After my escape, a Sunday afternoon, on my way back home, I stopped at a supermarket to buy food for my family. I was harassed in a supermarket parking lot in Silver Spring by the evil. He took my bag and kicked me so bad that I was not able to breathe. He took my cell phone, and I fought with him to get it back. My cell phone fell on the floor, and the bag got open. I was able to get my cell phone and called the 911 police; when the police came, the evil had run away. The police was able to catch him and brought him to the crime scene. The police asked me what happened: I talked to them about the harassment. The police advised me to file for a protective order from the court. I went to the court the next Monday to file for the protective order. The clerk of the court asked me if I had a pending case: I told her that my divorce case was pending. She went into the system and found out that the divorce was not filed. I was able to get a temporary protective order. Two weeks later, I was in court with the evil, where I got the final protective order.

I called my lawyer two days after the court to let him know that he took my money and did not file for my divorce. In fact, the clerk of the court told me that there was no record of a divorce in my name at the courthouse. I requested my money back because he had already took my eight hundred dollars. In fact, the same lawyer was trying to date me by setting an appointment with me at his house. The same lawyer, one night, called me at around 11:30 p.m. to tell me that he wanted me to come to his office because he had a gift for me that I would never forget. I suspected that the lawyer had plotted with the father of my children to hurt me or to kill me. Moreover, the lawyer had tried many times, when I went to his office, to have sex with me. After all those scenes, I requested to the lawyer that I wanted my money back. He gave me the eight hundred dollars in three months.

In December of 2004, after months of stress—because I was going through many abuses, like the physical and verbal; and many controls like financial, friends, and family; and because I was also hurt in my self-esteem and confidence by the evil—I was able to get the key to my apartment. In fact, for many months, I was not able to sleep enough because I was scared for my life and the life of my children and father. I also remembered that I was very scared to go home after school and sleep in the same bed with the evil.

I started to move my stuff little by little after I got the key to the apartment. One Friday, I was done with the moving; my father my children and I left the apartment to the evil. I had only taken my clothes, school supplies, my father's stuff, children's stuffs, and some blankets. My father and I, after the escape, went to the store to buy my kitchen supplies and the necessary equipment and furniture that I needed. I remembered that during the last part of the moving, which was to take my father and my children, it was during peak hours and I was not able to get to the apartment where I used to live with the evil before 4:00 p.m., which is usually the time when the evil came home. I was able to get there only at 5:00 p.m. Lucky for my father, children, and me that the evil was not home yet; therefore, we were able to move without fighting for the children's custody. I also recalled that during my life with the evil, the children's educational life was very behind compared to people of their age group. The evil, when he was with the children because he was avoiding responsibility, would put noninstructional music for the children to listen. It was only after my escape that I was able to enroll my children in the head-start program for them to get to the same level as other children. I slept like I had never slept for a long time. I did not have any bed or mattress; I slept on the floor in my room, and my father also slept on the floor in his room.

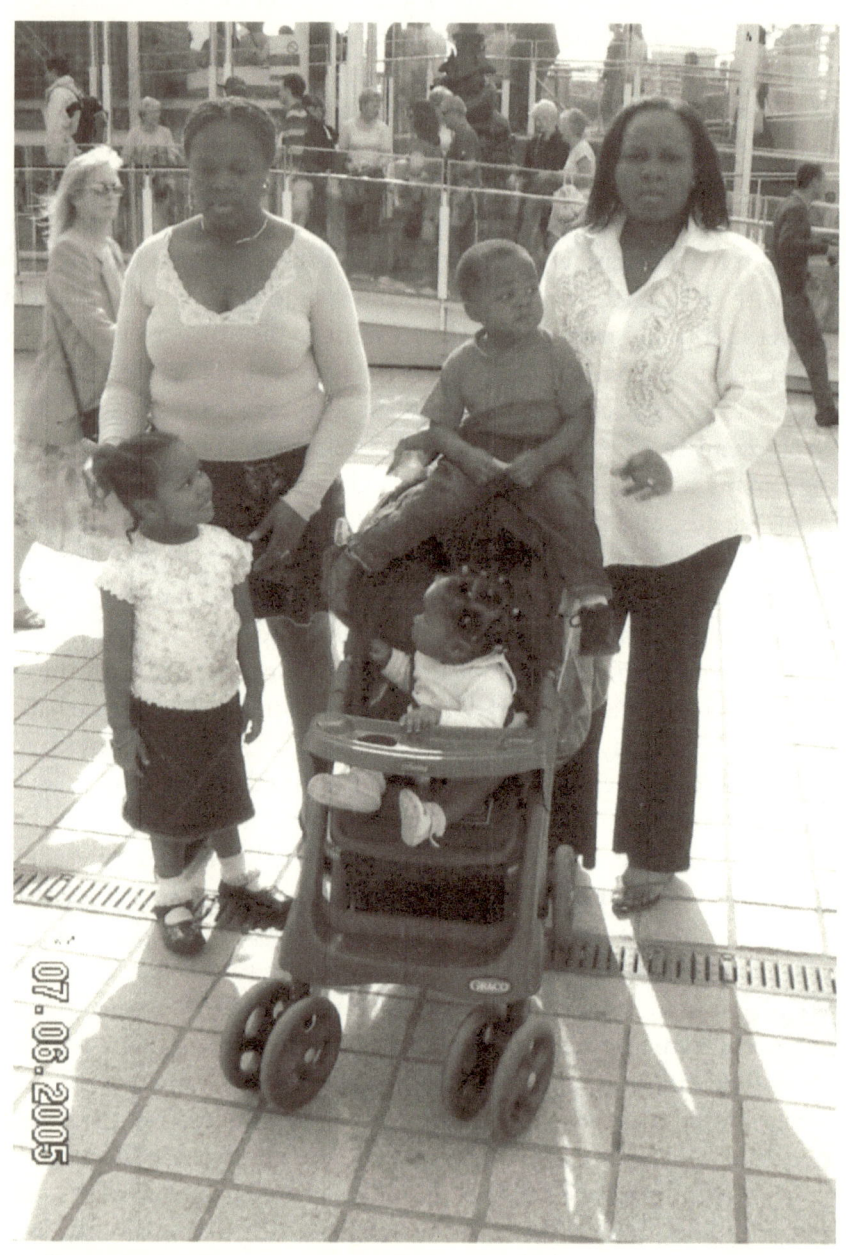

Annie T Djoum during her visit to sister Liliane Kom in London with children Ange and Ryan and niece Leandra.

**Annie T Djoum during her visit to sister
Liliane in London with Calvin Njampou sister
partner and my kids Ange and Ryan with niece Leandra and Dodo.**

Chapter 12:
My Visit to My Sister Liliane in London

After my escape from the evil, my father—because he had been in the USA for more than one year—had to go back to Cameroon to see his other children, my mother, and his family. My plan with my father was that my mother had to come after my father got back to Cameroon to help me with the children so that I can have trustable company and go to work and school. In order for me to have some vacation and some time off, I decided to visit my sister in London and offer some vacation to my kids. I asked my sister if she can help me with the children for two months. She agreed. In May of 2005, my father went back to Cameroon. I went to London with my children. I was in London for three weeks. During my stay in London with my sister, it was very helpful to me because I talked to my sister about everything that I went through during my stay with the evil. I was also able to have some vacation because I was also able to have some time off from school and work. I visited my sister's friends in London, and also, I visited the city of London. I was in London for three weeks. After those three weeks of stay in London, I came back to the USA because I was taking a summer class, and I went back to work.

Unfortunately for me, the plan to bring my mother to the USA did not work because the visa was denied to my mother at the embassy of the USA in Cameroon. The reason was that when she came to the USA, she stayed for more than five months on the six-month visa that she got. I went back to London at the end of August to get my children because my sister was able to help me just for two months. My daughter had to start her class in the head-start program, and also, I had to start my program in the surgical technologist program at Montgomery College in Takoma Park, Maryland.

Because I was able to escape and the evil knew that he had lost the opportunity for me to give him the green card, he continued to think of ways to hurt me. He went to the circuit court, where he filled the petition that he don't know where the children were. I went to the court and told to the judge that the children will come in August. The evil was not paying any child support at all.

I went back to London in August to take my children. I came to the USA with the children.

Chapter 13:
Custody Battle with the Evil

I came from London with the children and was just by myself in the USA, with an admission at a health science program, my rent to pay, and my bills that I had to pay for. I knew that if I let myself down, the evil and his followers would declare victory. I called one of my friends who told me that her mother could babysit for me. I was giving my children to their mother, who was living not far from my school. After three weeks of her mother babysitting my children, she found another job where she was well paid. I was faced again with the babysitter problem for my children because I had to go to school and work during the weekend, and also, my daughter had to go to school. Lucky me—after days of intensive search, I was able to get a babysitter across the street of my building.

I filed at the court because the evil was not paying child support. We went to the court, and he was handcuffed by the police. He went to jail and paid the money that he owed me. Because the evil had weekend visitation with the children at that time, he would come late at the restaurant where the judge decided that we needed to exchange the children in. He would, instead of bringing me the children on Sunday, bring them on Monday because he wanted to mess up my school and work schedule.

I went to the court for two years, where I was able to get the sole legal and physical custody of the children. I remembered that the judge asked me if the evil was not dangerous to the children, because she did not want to give him the visitation rights for the children. I told her no. The evil got the weekend visitation for the children.

My grand-mother, Margueritte Simo with great grand son
Ryan and Ange at Ange's dance party with mother
Annie T Djoum 2 years after my escape from the evil.

Annie T Djoum with grand-mother Margueritte Simo
at my graduation ceremony from College with son
Ryan and daughter Ange.

**My grand-mother Margueritte Simo with great
grand-children Ange and Ryan.**

Chapter 14:
My Grandmother's Visit To The USA.

Before my father went back to Cameroon, I sent an invitation letter to my mother and grandmother to come to the USA. My mother did not get the visa for the reason that I mentioned earlier. Only my grandmother got the visa. My grandmother, before coming to the USA, went to visit her daughter, my aunt in Paris. After her four months of stay in Paris, my grandmother came to the USA, where I was waiting for her. I was therefore able to get some help with the children because I was going to school and working.

My grandmother Marguerite was a very big help for me because I have a family member and a very trustable friend. I remembered that, one week end, when we went to drop off the children for the weekend visit, the evil totally ignored my grandmother. My grandmother had been here with me in the USA for more than four years. She was able to witness all the misery that the evil made me go through during the visitation. During my grandmother's visit to the USA, I was able to have a social life because I was in charge of the cultural section of the meeting of people of my village, Bayangam, in Cameroon. I was also able, with my grandmother's help, to graduate from Montgomery College, where I got my associate degree in applied science and general education.

My friend Dr. Anne-Marie Moukala Cadet and me
during a visit to new York.

Chapter 15:
My Visit to My Best Friend,
Dr. Anne-Marie Moukala
Cadet, in New York

In November of 2008, my grandmother, my children, and I traveled to New York. I drove my car for more than eight hours to go to New York. During our trip, I got lost many times but was finally able to get there safe with the children. We also stopped in Philadelphia with my grandmother and children, where we were able to visit the city and eat in a restaurant with my family. I also remember that that day, it had rained too much during the trip; therefore, it was very difficult for me to drive safely. We were able, after all those problems, to get to New York safely, where I met my best friend of more than twenty years. I was able to stay with my best friend, her husband, and children for three days. I spent the Thanksgiving with her family and her. It was very exciting to meet a friend that I did not see since 1990 in Cameroon. We ate turkey and mashed potato during Thanksgiving. I was also able to visit her children's school and the hospital where she worked before. I was also able to visit the town where she lived before. After three days of stay with her, I travelled back to Maryland with my children and grandmother. The trip was very helpful for me because my friend and I talked about many things. In Cameroon, my friend was like a sister to me. The trip was important because I was able to lift my spirit up.

Chapter 16:
Divorce Battle with the Evil

In July 2004, I went to the circuit court in Rockville, where I filed for divorce. I was able to hire a new lawyer, who took care of all the divorce procedure. After many meetings with the lawyer, I was able to get a file open for my divorce case. I met with the lawyer in his office to talk about my case with him, and after the first meeting, he told me that the judge could grant me a divorce. Because my lawyer was a pro bono lawyer and also because I have children with the evil, I was in court for more than two years with the evil. I also remember that before my grandmother came to the USA, I had to hire two babysitters: one during the week and the other one for the weekend. I was going to school during the week and was working during the weekend to support my family.

I also remember that we went to many educational meetings at the courthouse about parenting and divorce. After two long years of moral abuse by the evil, after my escape, I was able to get an absolute divorce. I was so blessed to have my grandmother Margueritte here in the USA with me.

Chapter 17:
The Evil Ways of Doing:
The Physical Abuse, the Verbal Abuse,
And Different Controls

After my escape, a Sunday afternoon, on my way back home from work, I stopped at a supermarket to buy some food for my family. I saw the evil coming from a corner; I thought that he came to say hi to me. Because I think that when you have been treated so badly like that by someone and you are able to escape, life with that person should not be a battle. One more time, the evil showed me that he was the evil. The evil came to me and harassed me. He kicked me so bad that I was hurt because I was not able to breathe. He took my handbag and my cell phone, and I fought back to get it back. My cell phone fell on the floor and my bag got opened; all my stuff fell on the floor. Therefore, I called the 911 police. When 911 arrived at the harassment place, the evil had run away. The police was able to catch him and bought him to the scene place. The police asked me what happened: I talked to them about the harassment. The police advised me that I should file for a protective order.

During my stay with the evil, I was living a very miserable life because he was not supportive of my work, education, or whatever I would try to achieve. He was making fun of my master's thesis that I got in Cameroon by telling me that I was doing nothing with that in the USA. He was also making fun of my studies at Montgomery College by telling me and friends that I was studying English. When I was working as a bosser in a restaurant, he would make fun of my job by telling my father that his daughter was working as a bosser in a restaurant. I was living with the evil with a very low spirit that was also affecting my health and my physical well-being: lucky me that my father was with me at that time to support and encourage me.

I was also beaten many times by the evil. The first time was when I asked him why he took one hundred dollars from my account. He beat me to death and apologized later. This was the reason why I did not call the police. The second time that I was beaten by the evil was when my aunt who paid for my travel ticket to come to the USA came to visit us. I asked him to buy a present for my aunt. He beat me because of that. The third time was one night, at around 11:00 p.m., after he came back from work at the restaurant. He noticed that I sent money to a friend to help her because her daughter was sick. He beat me to death in front of the children. I knocked at the wall to ask for help from the neighbor, but nobody came. In fact, the evil took my cell phone so that I could not call the police, and the home phone was disconnected on the wall. The front door was closed by the evil. My son and daughter were crying; the evil has no compassion and remorse. The evil was making fun of me; the more I was crying, the happier the evil was. In self-defense, because I was feeling like I was dying, I scratched the evil; after many scratches, the evil let me get of off the apartment. I went barefoot to the public station and called 911. I remember that my eyes were red with blood; my hand and face was hurting. When the 911 police came, two male police, the evil was sitting on the sofa in the living room with my son, whom he was holding in his hands. I was the one blamed because he had blood on his face. They asked him if he wanted them to bring me to jail. The evil said no. The police told him, "I saw that you were fighting together."

The evil always said to my father that we would do whatever he wanted us to do. His strength was that I was in this country that I prayed too much and worked so hard for in Cameroon to get this opportunity. I remembered that when I was doing my bachelor's degree, I used to go from embassy to embassy to look for a scholarship because I wanted to have one that will pay for my medical school and PhD. I was tired of being taken care of by my parents. Lucky me, I got not only a scholarship but an immigrant visa to be in a wonderful country that valued life and people's needs. But unfortunately, the evil was on my way to bring me down and mess up my dream and happiness and to put an end to my life. I also remember that the evil told one of our common friends that he beat me to death, and I was the one blamed by the police because the police wanted to bring me to jail.

I also recall that after me being harassed in a store parking lot, I got the protective order. A few days after the harassment, I called child protective service and brought my son to the doctor. My son told the doctor that Daddy cut his feet with the scissors. The doctor wrote it in my son's chart and told us that he would call child protective service. I called child protective service after the doctor's office to tell them that they needed to call the doctor to get the medical record. I waited one week and called child protective service again. They told me that the doctor never gave them the medical record. I went to the doctor's office for the record; another doctor who was working with my children's pediatrician told me that the chart was not in the office. My conclusion is that the doctor and the evil planed to hurt my son and say later that I was the one who did it. In fact, the weekend that my son's feet was cut, the evil told me that he would, on Sunday, give me only my daughter and not my son because he wanted to go to see the doctor on Monday with my son.

After all those events, the doctor was very embarrassed. When I was going to his office with the children for the annual physical check up. He also threatened me by saying that I did not bring my daughter to the doctor for three years and that I can go to jail for that. He wrote in my daughter's chart that I did not bring her to the doctor for three years. Before I changed the doctor to get a new one, I requested a copy of my children's medical record. In my son's medical record, the page where my son's feet were cut was still inside.

I also remember that the evil used to make fun of me by telling me that the lottery saved me, because he said that even with my master's, I would have been selling in his shop. Before my escape, all my documents and the children's documents—like green card, social security card, marriage certificate, birth certificate—were stolen by the evil. I did not have any control of all those documents. Lucky me—one day, the evil came and forgot to leave his bag in the car as usual. He brought the bag and put it on the table in the living room. I woke up at nighttime to get some water. I saw the bag and took all my documents and children's documents.

I recall also that the evil used to make my father, who had high blood pressure, cry by telling him that he had to go with his daughter because he was too old for me. He also told me that I had to do like my sister Liliane by finding a young partner of my age. He also told me that it was okay with him for us to divorce. The only deal that he wanted was for me to go with my children and for him not to pay me the child support. I can also recall the lack of interest that the evil had for me. Two months after my escape from the evil, to make fun of me, he sent me a bag of gifts from the postal service. The bag had clothes and shoes that were sent to me as a gift. The evil did not even know my clothes size or shoe size.

The evil is a very controlling person and also has demonic ways and methods. When he noticed that I was with friends or someone, he would look at my cell phone to get the person's contact. He would meet the person and would say bad things about me to her or him so that the person would hate me and I would experience loneliness. He moreover would look at all my friends and tell them that he would give them one hundred thousand dollars for them to convince me to give him the green card.

I also remember that the evil was someone very controlling and selfish. I remember that when I was coming to the USA, the evil told me that when I got there, I didn't have to open an account. I needed to wait him to come here for us to open a common account. The evil was also someone who had no foundation when he does his stuff. When I was student for my photography class, the teacher requested a professional camera. I bought one. The evil was unhappy because the camera was expensive. In fact, I was using my money and not his money. The evil was someone who liked to divide people. I remember that when my father was here, he wanted to divide us, because he told my father that I was sending money to my aunts in Africa. Because he knew that my father did not have a good relationship with my aunts, he used that method to make my father not love me. The evil also used to tell me that the fight would be very long. The evil also told his friends that he was a bee and would bite them. The evil, when he goes to store, would steal and change the tag and prices on the items.

After I came back from Belgium, where I was very sick and stopped my studies, my mother, who is my best friend and the person that I trust the most and who loves me more than anyone in this world, was making fun of me because she and my father spent too much money for my studies in Belgium, and I came back to Cameroon without any diploma. For me to get my mother's love and attention and to be the child that she loved the most, I started to buy clothes, jewelry, and making cake which I sold during my leisure time while going to school. I sold it and gave some money to my mother, for me to have a place in her heart and their house. I also wanted to show my mother that I was not a lazy person. I was doing well in school. When I met the evil, he came to visit me at night at the university campus. In fact, I met him when I was going to my master's thesis classes. After my master's degree studies, I was looking for scholarships and was also planning to continue my studies in Cameroon, if I didn't have one. I told the evil that I wanted to open a shop where I can sell clothes and other stuff. He came to my parents' house and took my money to open the store. He came the second time and took some money.

Chapter 18:
The Reason Why I Am Still Standing on My Feet Today

When I was living in the USA with the evil, I had the opportunity to observe him closely to see who he was. I knew that because I was more educated than the evil, he was jealous. The evil wanted also to mess up my life by treating me so bad, because he wanted me to become homeless. He used to make fun of me by telling friends that I had no family members in the USA. The evil wanted also to steal my dream to become an American citizen. He was also jealous of my plan to go to school and get a medical degree/PhD. I am still standing today because I knew that if I became a U.S. citizen, I can file to bring people that love me unconditionally—like my mother, father, and sisters—to the USA legally so that I can have a strong support group and also help my sisters to go to the best universities in the world and to be in the best country in the world. I did not let myself get depressed or traumatized, because I did not want to lose my children; moreover, I did not want my children to be educated by the evil, because he has no go manners and he acts like a child of the street.

Chapter 19:
Conclusion

In closing, my book was written to educate women, the society, parents, counselors, homosexual couples, lesbian couples, and heterosexual couples. My book describes the warning signs of the evil and evil ways of acting.

In the research of happiness and family life, because I believe that marriage is the foundation of society, my self-esteem and feelings have been hurt by the man whom I thought I would raise my children with. I was victim of many abuses by the evil. The evil's interest since Cameroon was to have his green card and then abandon me with the children. Without my family's support—without my mother, grandmother, and father—I would have not been alive today.

In summary, these are the evil ways: financial control, physical control, creating enemies between friends and family members to have the control and use you, big liar, not willing to learn from nobody, full of jealousy, has no compassion, opportunistic person, someone who will destroy people's reputation, someone who will be constantly looking for a way to hurt you. The evil would hurt you so bad that you will be morally and physically weak. The evil is not supportive of your studies.

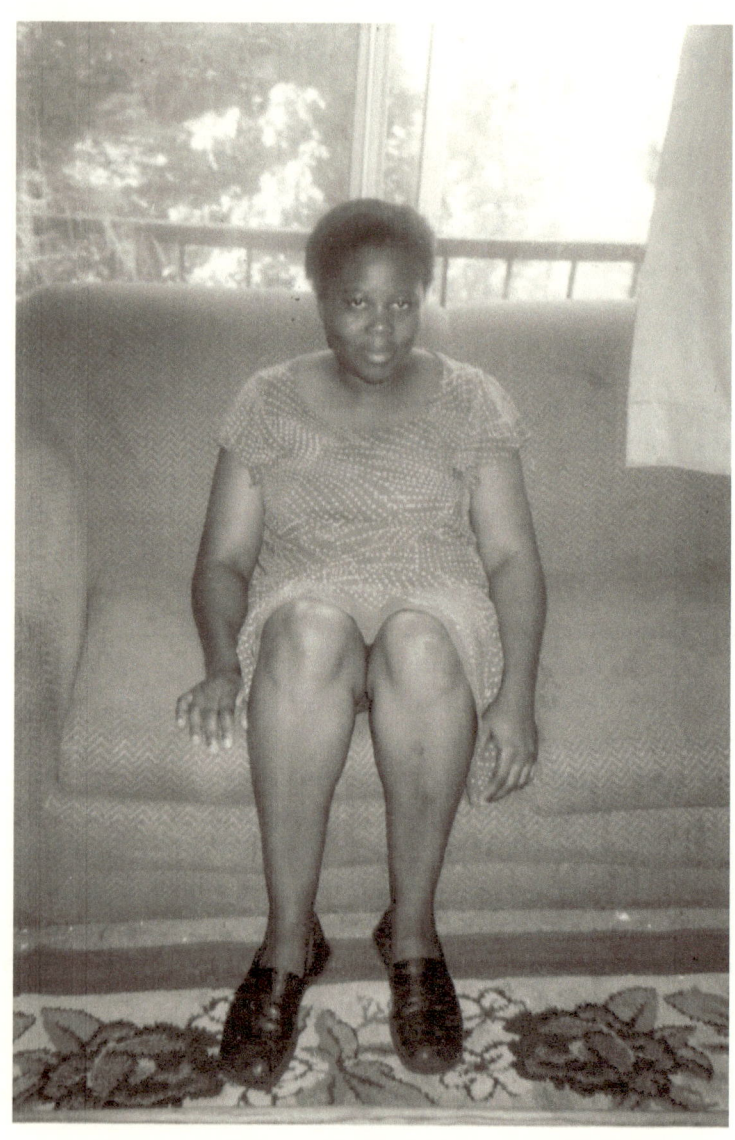

**This is what Annie T Djoum Looked like during
her brief marriage to the evil**